CORE

poems

DENISE MILLER

Willow Books, a division of AQUARIUS PRESS

Detroit, Michigan

CORE

Copyright © 2015 by Denise Miller

All rights reserved. No part of this publication may be reproduced, stored in a retrieval system, or transmitted in any form, or by any means, electronic, mechanical, recording, photocopying or otherwise without the prior written permission of the publisher.

Editor: Randall Horton
Cover design: Denise Miller

ISBN 978-0-9961390-5-2
LCCN 2015955188

EMERGING POETS & WRITERS SERIES
WILLOW BOOKS, a division of AQUARIUS PRESS
PO Box 23096
Detroit, MI 48223
www.WillowLit.net

Credits: "Supper" first appeared in Dunes Review, Winter 2007-08; "Shutter" and "Clean" first appeared in *African American Review* 42.3-4; "Hiring", "When They Sent Me Home", "Closing" and "Purpose" appeared in *american ghost: poets on life after industry* from Stockport Flats Press, 2011; "Leave" and "Which Stars" appeared in the December 2013 issue of *BLACKBERRY: a magazine*, and "Afterbirth" and "Origin Story: a braided triolet" were finalists for the 2014 Alexander and Doris Raynes Poetry Competition and appear in *Union*, the competition's anthology.

CONTENTS

Floors and Fittings...5

Communion..6

Miracle..7

Story, Tell Me...8

Clean...9

Birth...10

Afterbirth..11

Supper..12

Leave..14

Which Stars? a braided aubade...15

Shutter...16

Semantics..17

Origin Story: a braided triolet..18

Hiring...19

Closing...20

Something..21

Together..22

re/casting: a ghazal...23

and I was the middle..25

the 15th & the 1st..26

100 acres & no mule...27

Son of A..28

Inherit, This	29
I've Never Been	30
This Line	31
When They Sent Me Home	32
On This Hot Line	33
And I Came Out	34
Foreman's Visit	36
Mm Hm	37
Still Living	39
Got Hired, Got Here	41
I	42
How Long?	44
Purpose	46
What Was She Doing?	47
So She?	48
Oil	49
Turn That Hog On, Let It Rock	50
Did You Want?	51
Song of Songs	52
What I Want You to See	53
Acknowledgments	54

Floors and Fittings

This is the house built on flat of scrap white
pine and sycamore— family, floored with chisel,

chainsaw, hammer. They faced the flat of walls,
lime plastered and plugged of breath by sand

and water too wet to bet the mortgage on. This
is the house built on sweat of potsherd women

whole as wood thinnings, and yet they rolled
the bones of great, grand and mother, fashioned

tongues as door with chisel, chainsaw, hammer—they
bet the rent on love-lack, and lack of love is what their

whetstone bent into its fittings, then strawed to broom
they jumped from heart to floor. This is the house built

with muddied-good intentions dried to vow stopped breath
and yet, and yet, they bet with chisel, chainsaw, hammer.

      So send a postcard just to the west of I do and yes
and there will be the house built
with chisel, chainsaw, and hammer.

Communion

Saturday morning sun streaks
through stained glass, slanting

gold across red carpet, as if God
gathered up his glory and threw

it clean through the milky way to
split this steel gray morning. We

have already been to the furnace.
Stirred coals until they coughed

like a young boys lungs after a puff
on his first cigarette while we waited

for the church's coffee colored walls
to warm. Although it's nothing new to

us, this once monthly ritual of pouring
grape juice into glasses, placing glasses

into round, silver trays; I round the corner
of the pew and pause, preparing to meet

God. At the altar, we place silver trays
piled with small glass cups cupping the

blood of Christ. Sit them on the wooden altar.
Then whisk starched white sheets across

so quickly, that the flap of fabric
catches air and for a moment, flies.

Miracle

For a moment, I am flight.
She is right. My slip of stream
gleams gold instead of smoke.

And she is also right to sight me
in the shined sweep of sunlight, instead
of in the scratch and spill of ink.

They are choking her with Sunday
stories— they are splintering me
into thorn and nail and rails of wood.

When she rounds this corner I could turn
her wine back to water, undo the fiction
that makes her totter. Instead, I breathe
in her belief and exhale fabric into wings.

Story Tell Me

                                                                                                   :her

that cellophaned tenets turn to heartwood. Story, sell me that this body
is a trunk, sunk deep into its own soil. Convince
my fingerprinted memory that when roots coil skin
that it isn't the paradoxed end of living. Only
the lip of hope that births bleak into a beginning rinsed
of snake and apple and eve-figged sin.

                                                                                                   :god

Story, tell her that love is a mouth, bell shaped and coward-quiet
grioting god into truth—loose as lightning
flying into sunlight. Story, whisper wildly
that tonight love is a verse that eviscerates silence—
a fairytale where the beanstalk is really a tree that rises
in its rooting—right now in her back yard-deep and bark-skin winding.
Story, spell her a tale of tears turned to taproot grown from unbinding—
salted seeds split from the tip of her tongue, growing   defiant.

Clean

I live in my mother's back yard. In a house
as yellow as summer lemons and just as sour

beyond the pith inside. Two sons and three
daughters have fallen from between my legs

like water. I am quick as the click of high heels
on nighttime pavement and have mimicked my

mother's week-long work in white women's kitchens.
But, I have refused the rough knees knocked out

on the rub of linoleum and wood by bending low
when they came in to see me shine their floors.

I never got down on my knees for white folks
or God either.

Birth

She says I fell from between her legs like water,
but I know I was no river. I wasn't rushing in to life
because I've never rushed into anything.

I know instead, that I trickled creek water slow,
threading length of birth canal to daylight. Feet
first probably, to measure the give and take of ground.

And all the while I wound, I was testing her pace since all her
life she sounded all grace and click and tick-tock movement
while I sounded shuffle and seep and drip-drop stream.

Afterbirth

                                                          :mother

                                    I saw her as sheath of bat
                                    wing. At 3 or 5 of 4 or maybe 2
                                    she was transparent and still, until
                                    the singing sling of Orion's belt blew
                                    her away from this, our second skin.

                                    I could see her lift at the corner of my
                                    eye and knew she wanted to bring
                                    me in. Wanted to fold me in
                                    the flap of her hurt-shaped hollow, so

:daughter

I bent my boneless sorrow into bow
string, forged my steel-tipped ache
into the break where arrow meets sin.
I wanted to shape my heart-skin
to be the quiver she bears me in.

I wanted her to meet me again—wanted
her to greet me as bat wing or know
me as the singing sling of orion's belt.

Supper

Light streaks across black sky tonight like colored
ribbons blown straight by wind. The air's so
still, seems earth forgot to breathe, again.

I set down the bowl of snap beans I am splitting
for tomorrow's supper on the wooden porch slats
and watch the night shape your saunter to the bottom step.

You are straight and healing as milkweed.

Come to New York with me, you say. I hear a black
man can dig out more of a life in those wide streets
than he can in these dark Ohio valley coal mines.

Your words mount the steps my father built as you wear
a grin so contagious that it curves from the corners of your
cheeks like creek water. You promise—

We could leave tomorrow.

I am sitting stiff backed on a rough-hewn
rocker. My baby's cries slip through the screen
door and blow the wind right out of me. I watch

moon light fall to earth like ashes from the roof
of a burning house. I am black. A woman. Aged
twenty-five. Mother of three. Widowed.

The night air still holds stiff as silence.

The fingers of my right hand stroke the slip of bean still folded
in its palm. I snap one stringed edge, the other, then my thumb
and forefinger split the bean swiftly in two. I have always loved

the beans that grow out back beyond the buckeye trees.
Just now I know, you will pack one small bag tonight,
full of blue trousers and white shirts.

Tomorrow, I will bake ham for me to eat with these green beans for supper.

Leave

We could leave tomorrow. Could slip
off alley dust like the slate blue work shirt
I skin off mid-threshold every night.

Baby, if you are a sassafras tree in flower—
I am dandelion all gone to seed. Here,
all the life gets blown out of me.

Which Stars? a braided aubade

                                                                    :she

Since the rising points of stars sit sure, there's no need
to right ourselves on morning. This slightly southern
moon albumins the tips of grass, egg white— when I
was young, I used to pinch the belly of a firefly, lay its
light on my marriage finger then let it trail my linger
into midnight. Now, the only breath that feeds me
is stirred to wind by the shelled song of cicadas.

                                                                    :he

Baby, each day our risings and settings could be
due east or south of this nowhere. Honey, instead
of being pulled by tide, we could make our own light—
could site ourselves in the spark of train to track. You
got to know; I can't go back to young. Cause then all I
wanted was to run straight through night to morning.

Shutter

When my granddaughters strain to snap
my picture, I turn my head away so
suddenly that the slap of it shapes
their smiles into small, black o's.

There was a time, that hours saw me
stop in mirrors to see my reflection,
that mornings saw me slice a perfect
charcoal c under each eye, then slowly
trace my smile red. There was a time
when my legs were thick with possibility,
that I would stop along roadsides to pick
cattails and search for my silhouette in sunlight.

This is not the first time I have refused
to see myself. There was a time before
marriage to a man whose fingers held the neck
of a whiskey bottle with more gentleness than when
they gripped my own throat, a time before six boys
were born out of me, only to be made in their father's
image, a time before cushions cradled the familiar
curve of bodies, my husband's at the center of our bed
and mine on the couch that I mark as the first time,
when I, mirror less, veiled my face in white lace, then
closed the door to my father's house and opened
it to my husband's without looking.

semantics

it wasn't a whisky bottle's neck i nuzzled.
it was the stiff slick of a peony. just add this
to the things she got bottle-necked between
what I shoulda been and could never be. She

was word-raised while i grazed on auto grease
and miner's dust. she bent abc's into some kinda
damn verse— so yeah, i buried xyz's in her throat.
see, i was mechanic and she was engine—all piston

and ring. and when i oiled her—
bone and breath,
boy could she sing.

Origin Story: a braided triolet

                                                                                                    :she

It was always the whiskey bottle's neck.
The fact that father's fingers figure eighted mother's
adam's apple, pushed "i do" from these lips liquid as breath.
It was always the whiskey bottle's neck.
I know you also got birthed from death.
I know your daddy grabbed the throat of   your mother.
It was always the whiskey bottle's neck—
the fact that daddy's fingers figure-eighted mother's.

                                                                                                     :he

how you know my nicotine and lovers
ain't fruit from the family tree i watched my daddy plant?
how you know i don't wanna be more than the fists of my father
how you know my nicotine and my lovers
ain't the whiskey-wet haint that hovers
in my sons whose madness cuffs their kid's hands?
how you know my nicotine and lovers
ain't the fruit from the family trees I watched my daddy's plant?

                                                                                                :togeth

how you know?
We can't.

Hiring

They lined us up daily. 10 or more men
outside the supervisor's office window.

Some of us, standing straight as whitewashed
fence posts, others as solid as the dark space

between rungs. All of us stiffing our spines
with the hope we'd be hired, while we were

measured day after day by a yard stick that
didn't exist. A line of 10 men whose legs turned

into question marks were pulled to paychecks
or pushed further to poverty by the point

of the supervisor's finger. He could tinker
with our futures in an Ohio Valley where it

was either steel or coal that put food on tables.
We couldn't name the criteria, so he kept

white men and their children seeing sunlight
while the few black men who made the cut, bent

themselves in half below ground. Once we got
in, we were in it. 300 feet deep at least and up

to our shins in water and rock dust with just enough
to depend on us above ground to keep us down under.

Closing

For years, the rumors didn't scare me. I knew
there was still 50 or 60 years of raw material to haul
out that could fuel me from age 21 to pension.
Besides, we had struck before and survived. Once,
we miners fed our families 109 days on fish and deer.

But this was different. It was devastating. I had worked coal
seams so steady that they stretched back to our father's and
their father's before them. Most of us went underground so young
that it felt like we had exchanged graduation caps for hard hats

to work a job that was supposed to be as stable as the bolts we
used to steady the tons-heavy coal ceilings with. See, I had spent
twenty years in shafts as short as my ten year old daughter where I
learned to go in safe. Coveralls, steel-reinforced boots, hard hat, light.
Stayed alert while my body measured time in the constant

chew, haul, bolt, scoop, chew, haul, bolt, scoop of the system.
Had lunched and hunched in a place where everyday it was completely
life or death. So it was impossible to believe that I would ever need to
reinvent myself. Hard to conceive that coming out could be what killed me.
I was a coal miner. Could see in light as thin as a pencil line but now,

with Y&O's doors closing, I couldn't see my future. But I searched
anyway. Found an opening 50 miles from home and applied. Felt
a high school education wouldn't make me one of the 87 hired
for a factory job. With 10,000 applicants whose resumes were weighty
while mine was light as coal dust, I knew I would have to trust God. So,

five months and no call found me steadying myself on scripture. Mining
bible page by page like I was mining pillar to post, prayer picking
up pieces of my spirit like loose coal. But God's promise pushed me six
months from last unemployment check to plenty.

Something

There is nothing here. Honest. Your Ohio Valley
is silent and choking; coal dust caked on a nineteen
year-old miner's lungs. It buries people.

Turns spirit to cinder and some of 'em don't
see it. Buries me too, but all I can do is
breathe it in, between I married you and again.

The first time, I was twenty-something.
A divorced mother. You were twenty-
something, Widowed. Needing

a mother for your daughters. We both
were there. Twisting our twenties
like turnpikes into adulthood.

We were not good, together.
Conversations that should have been
easy, caught in the clink of glass on glass

until we found ourselves whiskey-wrought
and fighting. I lulled myself with cigarettes.
That slow burn was something I could count on.

And you? You found your forgetting flecked in
the fins of fish. Hooked them mid-swim in a boat
big enough for one bucket and one body, only.

And me? I still keep a little money stashed
so that wherever and whenever I reach,
I have just enough to get away.

Together

Some days I am a boat, big enough
for one bucket and one body only.
My skin, the thin that sails through silted
memories that bank at my soul's edge.

Those days, I paddle to the strip
mine's center—drop anchor. Breathe.
Then feel the catch and slide of insides
settling as I thread bait through crook

of hook. I drop line. Look life into
the hole that swallows. Some nights
we face each other—faces fringed
with the flesh of fist-heavy

fathers and the skin of mothers
stiff as the slick of punching bags.
Our eyes and mouths—the picture
perfect film of water.

Those nights, air ceases to exist.
Those nights I dream of breathing.
Those nights my ears become
the gulping gills of fish.

re/casting: a ghazal

:he

The smallmouth spirals its scales toward sun; my hook exposed.
Tail breaks silence's surface. I tug, life's fight exposed.

There are rocks I want to hook from strip mine's bed. Polish
pieces into flecked stars; set them in your ears, exposed.

But polish-cloth is fingers flexed to unclog float-coal.
And this dust, raked from rock stops our blast. These years, exposed.

Water, penny-colored replicates this memory:
Your ring-box mouth you closed, reappears. All hurt exposed.

You say my back's a boatbed you can't curve your spine to.
My back's planking's plumbed to your vertebral fears, exposed.

I am a boat, bow-bent with burdens newly exposed.

:she

Nights, I don't face you; turn body to dream unexposed.
I hold breath to halt love's surfacing. Keep hope unexposed

There is rock I want to split from strip mine's bed. Fracture
"now" from "maybe"; hide in cupboard corners, unexposed.

This drill bit is teeth that crack from tongue's private puncture.
This hope is water slowed by oiled thickeners unexposed.

Nights, I gill water's oxygen to blood
Scale lips to fit your lungs. Leave loving years unexposed.

Days, I surface sore from shape-shifting feet into fins
Slip thin boned scales from eyelids that keep fears unexposed

My cheek first breaks water, wields your silver hook—exposed.

:testimony

*the found poems in this section are adapted from two of the 300 pages of oral histories of Latino/as and African Americans in Saginaw, Michigan collected and compiled by Dr. Michelle S. Johnson in a project called Community Spaces of the Industrious.

and I was the middle—Found Poem #1 A.R.9-9-99

---

                   full name and   *date of birth*   *for the record.*

            Abdul   Raheem   Rashada.
                                             12-17-25.

born?

                                           Starkville, Mississippi.

           Starkville,
                                          Mississippi?
                  Yes.
Mother? Father?
                  Yes. father   farmer. just for himself. enough to support
his family of nine children.
eight brothers and sisters?
Yes.
Where   did   you   fall?   Oldest,
                                             youngest,
                                             middle?
                                             Exactly.

           Middle.

                                         It was, it was
                                         nine of us and I
                                         was the middle
                                         child. It was two
                                         boys older than me, two boys
                                         younger than me, two girls
                                         older than me and two girls
                                         younger than me.

           So when you said exactly . . .
                                           Yes.

the 15th & the 1st—Found Poem #2 A.R.9-9-99

---

farming? what kind of
        small   scale   just to support   his   family
                yes.
  cotton, corn   hay   . . . we raised
      peanuts,
  sweet potatoes Sugar cane molasses   hogs and my mother

    raised a lot of chickens and let's see. milk cows   sell the milk.
              that's how
  he would come by a little money   And then the
            15th and 1st
                  they would pay him   for the milk
                          twice a month.

100 acres & no mule—Found Poem #3 A.R.9-9-99

___

Did he own   *his*
    land?
    How much land   *was he*
        working?
   100 acres
  land.   And some of it was
                            pasture
               and some of it was
                          hay
   and   some   he farmed
           and some was
           wood or timber,   where the trees grow   .
               once in awhile
           buy the trees   cut them down.

Son of A—Found Poem # 4 A.R.9-9-99

How did your father acquire the 100 acres?

        Okay that's a story too. During slavery time   you

        know   slave master, some

        kind enough   to   will

        property

  to

        the

slaves

                when they die

    some slaves were like children and they would will . . . and

        so my fathers' grandfather a child of the slave master.

Inherit, This—Found Poem # 5 A.R.9-9-99

Do you remember
                  his name?
   My   fathers'
grandfather?

Um hum.
      Jerry
                      Tait.
      Jerry   Tait.

     a little boy, he was   small

when
     the
slaves
was
freed   or whatever. But anyway
       he
received

100 acres
he   inherit   this   land   you
see.
And
       was
divided between the children.

Between the nine?
     Between   the nine

I've Never Been—Found Poem # 6 A.R.9-9-99

So how old were you when you left Mississippi?
      23   years old   .I'm thinking.
So what was it like in Starkville when you left?
            when you left?   *Stark*   *ville?*
    Segregated bad, real bad.   And I was . . .
    I had to leave

     because   white people   crazy
   when
     you were man enough   to
    say
        no   to   them no   to   them no
to   them no   to   them
     you know. And so   I've   never been one
       to buckle to nobody,   I've never been

    I've   never
          been.

This Line—Found Poem # 7 A.R.9-9-99

―――――――――――――――――――――――――――

So you got a job at Malleable in 1949?
    Malleable   yes.
    what   was   it   like   *Malleable*
    1949?
                                          Real bad.

What kind of work were you doing?
    Real bad,   hook out man
             real   bad
    they call it the hot line   a big conveyor belt
    brought iron out of the foundry, had a long line heavy containers

          they   loaded iron in the foundry.

Was it hot iron?
    Yes
        hot
   iron   pulled iron   set   iron shook   a
   shake out   iron
                    loaded
       conveyor corner belt   dump it on this line   guys
  that
  would knock the … off place behind you   hook
           off
  with
  these iron hooks, hook the iron off   put it over   behind
  you supervisor constantly   telling you,   you
  taking
  off
as much iron as you can take off now,   you tell you
     another job be coming in   say well I'll put it over here
     you're already getting as much as you can get   but they could
     come in and if you don't do it
         they send you home.

When They Sent Me Home

Started as hook out man. Had to catch solar hot iron flares
mid-spin on conveyor belts; pile it accordin' to job.

It was hard. Hard. Hard. Me takin' off much iron as I
could. Heat makin' me want to take my own skin off.

But knowin' that South to North in '49 made my wallet
handkerchief thin, forced me to keep the foreman

behind me makin' sure my hookin' hand could catch each
job. Put it in its proper place so I wouldn't lose my place

when they sent me home. And they sent me home, plenty.
'Cause I couldn't see the justice in that job or any. White

men standin' like picket fence line with clipboards and ties
while black men stooped, shovlin' coal dust or soot-brushed

and burnin.' 15 years of workin' that kind of shift had me ready
for shiftin' to somethin.' While 10 more saw me grind, mill and

press; I was all the while stretchin' spirit from cinder so that after
a fair day's work, people would know I wasn't no workin' boy.

I worked the big wigs like I worked the line. Fixed what needed
fixin'— took off only what was mine and felt the bill-fold in my

pocket, 'cause it was the rock iron that steadied me.

On This Hot Line—Found Poem # 8 A.R.9-9-99

Let me ask one more question,   *on this hot line was it*
    mostly black folks   *and Latinos*   *or?*
    Yes,   yes,   yes,

It   was
    mostly blacks   and Mexicans   you
    know.
    Just mostly blacks you see   you
        see.

And I Came Out—Found Poem # 9 A.R 9-9-99

when you on the line and the line break down or something
they always had   some   little   dirty

job that they wanted you to do
always.
And do some little   dirty   detail   whenever   they
would
come get me for the detail,   some   little   nasty

   detail, then I would ask them   how you choose me

how you come   by
               me.

                                        because I'm black.
Oh   no,   no   no.

          You   getting
          me? No,   no,
                              no. I

say   you getting me   because I'm the younge
man?

So   he couldn't give me   no justification   for
getting me so I
tell him   get another man   see
          because I'm not
          the youngest man,   I know I'm not
                    the
youngest
man, I'm older than   the white boy over there,
I'm older than   these boys over here,
     I'm older than   these over here,
now how you choose me   see.

                So
that's
the
way
I
                would fight them   . So I would
fight.   I
did
                until I came out for 25 years.

And I came out in 1975.

Foreman's Visit

It's not the last time he'll pocket his hand to pat my
shine. He strokes my skin, eager like he's makin'
sho I'm still there in the same secret way his Saturday
woman's fingers feel for the familiar rough of linen
folded line-fine as chisel edge in my money pocket.

I have been rocked by his up and down of hip since
he started standin' the line and know that when he
holds my sweat stained skin, he is really holdin'
his anger. See, I know I am the armor
that keeps him from takin' off his own skin.

Mm Hm—Found Poem # 1: J.F. Interview 8-4-99

Where I would like to start. Do you remember   your full name, your date
born?

    Johnny Fifer that's
        F-i-f-e-r.

born?

        Mississippi. Canton.

born?

        3-27-41.

Do you remember   it
        well?

    Yeah, I remember. It was rough; we sharecroppers lived—
        passed.
    Just the way it was back then. Raised
        corn, cotton, beans, sweet potatoes, the whoschlak.
    You name it, we raised   it—raised
        a complete crop.

Who owned
        the land?

    John Witt—he had
        land
  as   far   as   the eye
        could   see.

That your family
        worked?

    No— we shared   so much. Each family had
    so much
    on this plantation. I would say   he had

   at least 10, 15 families.

Really?
   Yeah.
All black?
   Mm
      hm.

Still Living—Found Poem # 2: J.F. Interview 8-4-99

```
So        how many acres          your                    family
                work?
          just the three of us.  That's
                   my grandmother—

          Your grandmother                           you
                        and—
my first cousin.
                   we
                        30 bails of cotton
                                      a year
the farm                     outside
              Canton?
          It was outside of Canton, it was
                 Madison County,      20 miles from town. daughters
          would come home to visit. grandmother four daughters and one son.


Everybody                             living
                         now?
         just one             left. still
               living.


What year                       did your grandmother
                     die?
              Oh God— I'll have to get back to condense it. they all
         came home.                              after we
         buried my grandmother.
         got our packing           we had crops    and stuff
               you know we had to let
```

                Mr. John know,
    well he knew   what was going on.
      a   n   d   I
didn't want to leave
                        I
        had been with him   all my life   and   t h a t ' s
    the only one
                        I did know.
I was going to Saginaw,   my mother was over
        [t]here.

Got Hired, Got Here—Found Poem # 3: J.F. Interview 8-4-99

So   how long   had your mom been   here Saginaw?

My mother,   I don't know   exactly   how long. Yes I do

Because   [mother] she met him.and they [husband]

hiring at the Malleable Iron so he   came   over   got   hired

    the same day   that's how she ended

                          up over here.

I—Found Poem # 4: J.F. Interview 8-4-99

So then you came to Saginaw?
    1950   Yeah.
So what was that like?
        come from living out on a farm
        [to]   *basketball?*
        I played   we played   summer league
Hoyt Park and I ice skated
I was going to play   but had the job, I needed   m o n e y,
my mother couldn't,
        you know,
        things that I wanted   better clothes   stuff like that so
   I   said well   I was able
so when I got out of school   I just went   straight to the
cleaners   and   started working
        there, then I worked till they closed   until
                Marcella   got
pregnant,
after   she   got
pregnant   with   my   daughter

        then
           I
              had
        to
drop   out of school
      the little job that   I   had   it wasn't enough
      to—
             then I had the responsibility.

the plant.

Mr. Foley

I went to Mr. Foley and he hired me at the Malleable.

How Long?—Found Poem # 5: J.F. Interview 8-4-99

---

        work was, oh God   work   was   hard
            at the Malleable.
What were you doing
            out there?
        Dubberman.

      what's that?
        That's the hardest,   that's lifting molds,

            I   mean   60,   70

How long?   *lift them up*   *off*   *the belt?*
      How long?
Lift it from the mold machine to the belt.
    About 8 hours.   Or
            9, 10.   whatever   they
   working   you   do.
Was hot?   *Wasn't*
      it?
Hot, hot, hot, I mean red hot. That's why I say you had to have a purpose or family
or something in order to stay. You had to know what work were or something you
know. You couldn't just go in there and I got a job. You had to have something
to think about that makes you do this for 8 or 9 or 10 hours. But
      soon
    as   you   got home,   Hands swoll,
  take some   Epsom Salt, Mama ... and

   alcohol and rub them   down.
How long?   *So you would*
         lift them

            till I got ready to retire.

Purpose

You had to have something to think about made
you able to be duberman or shake out at the Malleable.
8, 9, 10 hours of crackin' cast from sand or pouring
3000 tons of melted metal a day while sweat swilled
slick into iron and flicked like fireworks on concrete.

There was no freedom in this. Black men goin' in, skin
all shades of Saginaw soil, then coming out darker than the coal
that heated the foundry. See, I had to find me a purpose. Somethin'
to keep me shiftin' mold to belt so that every second felt light
as liftin' bread to my daughter's mouth with my fingertips.

What Was She Doing?—Found Poem # 6: J.F. Interview 8-4-99

---

                              she had got in the shop there.

Now   *what was she doing*   *in*
                    the   plant?
        I   don't   know.   I   never
                     did
                     go to an open house over there.

So you don't   know
                         what
                    kind of work   she   was   doing?

        No.   Yeah.   No I never did. I just...I
                         wonder why. I never did.
        But I know   they working
                         a lot of oily stuff.

A lot
                                   ?
        Yeah   cuz   when   she   got   home   she
                         smelled like   oil.

So She?—Found Poem # 7: J.F. Interview 8-4-99

So she was on the line?
    Yeah.

Oil

There was no freedom in this. True, black men went in.
But black women shed dresses for denim—also, stood the line.
Some shook soot from strands of hair. I scraped oil from mine.
There are lines we've all walked. Some thin and straight as pencil
lines. Some dark and slued crude-thick. We walked both.

Graphite light in years—we laid the first scratch together. Backs
arched passion-straight on silver seats in the back of a '56
Pontiac Starchief. The second, we scrawled grief-bent. My belly
baby-full and yours binge-heavy on obligation. Then, we crossed them.

You, when you found your music mingled with the growl and hum
of motorcycle engines. And me—when my skin breathed blow-oil
sour in the space perfume should have been.

Turn That Hog On, Let It Rock—Found Poem # 8: J.F. Interview 8-4-99

```
69                          we would be stretched    as far as the eye
                            could see        so we
         would cut off      hit M-13         to
                            Saginaw.                 Big   Buck   and
         them keep straight         up       go      under
                                                     the underpass,
                            that's some beautiful noise, you hear
         Harleys.

By the time we get home              bugs on the windshield,
         eyeglasses        it's 3:00 or 4:00 in morning
                           and it's like music to your ears.  I tell you
50, 75. 100 bikes coming down.  I mean ya'll rolling. 95 miles an
         hour              heading home
that was
a beautiful sound.         And you                  tooling on.
         Turn that hog on          let it rock, his lady, his
                           wife. Sometimes I hate        that    I
         sold my bike.
```

Did You Want?—Found Poem # 9: J.F. Interview 8-4-99
_____

So did your wife   *ever*   *go*   *?*
     Oh no,   no,   no,   no. She couldn't stand.
     Those, those, those . . . in fact
                 my wife never did
get on the motorcycle
                   and she didn't
         like that either. She said   "no
                                            way
                                            in life
                                            I'm
                                       getting   on   that
    two
                 wheeler."

Now   *did you want*
                     her

                     to at first?
                 yeah. By that time   you know
                 we just
                        . . . we wasn't . . . maybe when
                 we first
                 got together   she probably   would
have   but by that time

Song of Songs

                                                                                                                             :John

I should have breathed you in. Should have flicked convention
from my mind, but the oil slicked pencil line image of you rockin'
sand from molds of iron thick as your thighs after your thighs
rocked me, melted all this man so deep into misery that these fingertips
forgot the trace of your breast as you breathed sleep deep after lovemaking.

Forgot you ever breathed "mmm, Johnny. My man" into this curve of neck.
Forgot you flicked eyes at me lust lidded and laced, lashes thick as fingertips.
Forgot that those yearning years sailed yawl-young in a line. Forgot those sweat
slick moments you were mine. Then, I melted into you, my thin-shouldered
Marcella. What I wanted was you, virgin thick Cella to always belly up behind,

trace your lace thin fingers along this broad, thick back. Girl, did you have to haul
and hoist like that? Did you have to? Did you forget I breathed next to you?
Marcella, you had to? You could'a rubbed fingers raw and melted our poverty
in the sterile smell of bleach and soapsuds, could'a been black and women and flicked
misery from our mouths while fitting white folks socks on twine twisted and hung into line.
But you flicked away my soul fist-handed instead of pulling me in with your fingertips.

                                                                                                                            :Marce

John, you used to be Johnny. But my Johnny got lost between the thumb and fore
of fingertips pressed into filter thick lips then crushed into the rough of cement
as we blew, smoke curved into line. But, what's real had slipped from my geography
long before ingot got breathed into steel. Long before this brow bled sweat-red
into bandanna and men flicked my femininity into flecks of ore. I melted—

melted dreams into 12 days on 12 days off— melted fingertips into molten metal.
The job flicked identity from fingerprints. Still, I was hope thick that we still breathed
the huh-huhhhhh breath of first kiss. I still sauntered the line between bills and everything
is possible. But responsibility's wrinkle already etched a line between us. I mirrored your
manhood across cast iron molds, melted your memory of the first time we breathed togethe
Melted the melody of your fingertips the first time you touched the thick between my thigh
My soft and sway and switch flicked.

                                                                                                                                    :they

John, while I struggled to dream without any pieces of good truth
to mix up hope with, you flicked the me still wanting to be your
song-drink, your long drink, your talking drum into the thick of failure.
Cella, we touched with bodies bruised by surviving instead
of tendering our sores with our fingertips.

What I Want You to See

Birds crash at the feeder, drop
beaked seeds like moments.
Every moment distils into this:

The gardener my son imagined he was. The cosmo
seed he planted but forgot to crack first. The seed

of the son I imagined buried in the clay-cracked
soil of my womb. The robin-egged blue of the room

that seeded my never imagining a son who would
never plant a garden and the garden that would never

be fed by the wet wheel of the mill in the step mother's
place that became the wipe of the drop on the back

of the hand of the grandfather who tendered the petal
soft skin of his wife like the gardener my never-son

imagined himself to be. Look.
This is what I want you to see:

The grandmother, never flower frail.
The grandfather, whiskey-wet handed.
The son, never planted.

The seed—
        broken but never blooming.

Acknowledgments

Thank you to my father Dennis Miller for his invaluable contribution to this project. The information about coal mining in the poems "Hiring" and "Closing" came from his experiences as a miner in Cadiz, Ohio (my hometown) from the 1970s and 1980s, where he and countless other miners worked deep underground in perilous conditions.

Thanks to Dr. Michelle S. Johnson. The found poems in this book are adapted from two iron foundry workers from the 300 pages of oral histories of Latino/as and African Americans in Saginaw, Michigan she collected and compiled in her project titled Community Spaces of the Industrious. The words in italics in the found poems are excerpted from the questions Dr. Johnson posed to each of the two participants. The rest of the words are the responses of the participants.

Denise Miller, born in Martins Ferry, Ohio, and raised in Cadiz, Ohio, is a Kalamazoo Valley Community College instructor, artist, poet, and community activist. She received a BFA from Bowling Green State University in Creative Writing and an MA from Central Michigan University. Her work has also been funded by an Emerging Artists Grant from the Arts Council of Greater Kalamazoo and the Gilmore Foundation. Miller is co-founder of Fire, (www.thisisfire.com), an arts and culture nonprofit in Kalamazoo that has as its mission to encourage and respond to people's desire for authentic expression. There, Miller started Creative Justice Press where she and a team of high school and college interns edited and published a national poetry anthology and the chapbook winner from the press' first international chapbook competition. Miller is also executive chef and owner of fuel vegetarian restaurant in Kalamazoo. Fire reflects Miller's belief that social and cultural awareness generate and sustain social justice.

Miller has been awarded a 2015 Hedgebrook Fellowship. *Core* is Miller's full length poetry collection. Other publications include poems in *Dunes Review; Michigan Writers Corner; Terror and Transformation Anthology, Wising Up Press; Just Like A Girl Anthology, GirlChild Press; African American Review; american ghost: poets on life after industry from Stockport Flats Press*; and *BLACKBERRY: a magazine*. For more information: www.makedo.weebly.com

www.ingramcontent.com/pod-product-compliance
Lightning Source LLC
Chambersburg PA
CBHW030458010526
44118CB00011B/999